ROCKET TO THE MOON

The Incredible Story of the First Lunar Landing

by Lisa M. Combs

illustrated by Robert F. Goetzl

Troll

BridgeWater Books

For GVC and TMC, whom I love to the moon and back.
—L.M.C.

To Mom and Dad, with heartfelt gratitude for your
unwavering support and encouragement.
—R.F.G.

Library of Congress Cataloging-in-Publication Data

Combs, Lisa M.
Rocket to the moon : the incredible story of the first lunar landing /
by Lisa M. Combs ; illustrated by Robert F. Goetzl.
p. cm.
Summary: Describes Apollo 11's journey to the moon, the landing of
the Eagle, and the moon walk of Neil Armstrong and Buzz Aldrin in July 1969.
ISBN 0-8167-6331-3
1. Project Apollo (U.S.) Juvenile literature. 2. Apollo 11
(Spacecraft) Juvenile literature. 3. Space flight to the moon
Juvenile literature. [1. Project Apollo (U.S.) 2. Apollo 11 (Spacecraft)
3. Space flight to the moon.]
I. Goetzl, Robert F., ill. II. Title.
TL789.8.U6C65   1999
629.45'4'0973—dc21   99-24917

People have always loved the moon from afar.

It's strong enough to make the waves that crash onto all the world's shores. For thousands of years it has helped sailors guide their ships and helped farmers plant their crops. Children from every country have pointed up at it and sung songs about it.

Since the beginning of time, people have loved the moon from afar. This is the story of the first human beings to meet the moon up close.

Neil Armstrong, Buzz Aldrin, and Michael Collins risked their lives to meet the moon up close.

On July 16, 1969, three men risked their lives on a dangerous and marvelous journey to the surface of the moon. These three men were Neil Armstrong, Buzz Aldrin, and Michael Collins. Neil Armstrong was the mission commander and the astronaut chosen to be the first man

to walk on the moon. Buzz Aldrin, the lunar module pilot, would walk on the moon with him. Michael Collins was the command module pilot. He would not set foot on the moon's surface but would pilot the spacecraft to the moon and back.

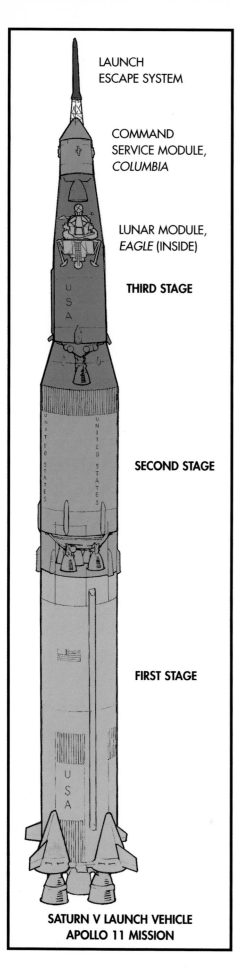

LAUNCH
ESCAPE SYSTEM

COMMAND
SERVICE MODULE,
COLUMBIA

LUNAR MODULE,
EAGLE (INSIDE)

THIRD STAGE

SECOND STAGE

FIRST STAGE

**SATURN V LAUNCH VEHICLE
APOLLO 11 MISSION**

The Saturn rocket that would take them there stood as tall as a building of thirty-five stories and weighed more than twenty-five jet airplanes put together. It was made of three engine stages, each of which would fall off after its fuel was used up. At the top of the rocket was the spacecraft, called *Apollo 11,* which had a command module, a service module, and a lunar module. The astronauts traveled in the command module. The service module held their food, fuel, and oxygen. These two parts together were named *Columbia. Eagle* was the name of the lunar module. When *Apollo 11* reached the moon, *Eagle* would break away from the rest of the craft and take Neil Armstrong and Buzz Aldrin to the lunar surface.

The tremendous rocket seemed almost alive as it was readied for takeoff. Huge puffs of steam billowed from it into the hot, humid air at Cape Kennedy in Florida. What was each man thinking as he got closer to the smoking giant? Did he look around him, wondering if he would ever see Earth again? Did he look up at the towering rocket and ask: "Will it really work? Will it really be able to land us on the moon and then bring us back to Earth?"

Were they afraid as they boarded the spaceship on top of the huge and powerful rocket?

Nearly two million people came to watch the amazing launch. One by one, the astronauts squeezed through the tiny hatch and took their positions inside *Columbia*. All the hustle and bustle of the morning came to a sudden end as the hatch slammed closed. The men sealed inside knew that the journey they had been dreaming of for years was finally about to begin.

The rocket blasted the spaceship with the three men inside it deep into space.

Armstrong clutched the abort handle, ready to pull it if the launch went badly. Ten, nine, eight, seven, six, five, four, three, two, one . . . The explosive liftoff could be seen, heard, and felt for miles around Cape Kennedy. A blazing trail of red-yellow flames streamed hundreds of feet behind the rocket as it blasted into space.

After just two and a half minutes, the powerful first-stage engine separated and splashed into the Atlantic Ocean. Four seconds later, the men were jostled about in their seats again as the second stage thrust them even deeper into space and fell away. The entire vehicle was now less than half its original size, with only the third-stage engine left of the once-enormous Saturn rocket.

The astronauts floated against the straps of their seats as weightlessness suddenly came upon them. Was it like the feeling you get when you're dreaming you can fly? The three men looked out the spaceship windows at the amazing planet they called home. They watched the horizon line begin to curve as they gradually traveled far enough away from the Earth to see its roundness. How did they ever concentrate on the jobs that needed to be done inside the spaceship while the beautiful blues, greens, pinks, and purples of our planet swirled miraculously outside their windows?

The astronauts saw the beautiful planet Earth outside their windows.

Less than three hours had passed since takeoff. The third-stage engine fired, placing the spaceship in orbit around the Earth. The craft circled the Earth one and a half times before the engine roared again, sending *Apollo 11* hurtling through space at 24,300 miles per hour. The spaceship burst out of the Earth's gravitational pull. It was headed for the moon.

For the last big task of the day, Michael Collins released *Columbia* from the third-stage rocket, which was holding *Eagle* in a special shell.

Michael Collins turned *Columbia* around and attached it to *Eagle* in a new position.

Incredibly, *Eagle* and *Columbia* were now separated from one another, zooming through space at the same speed on the same course! But when Collins pushed the control knob that was supposed to turn *Columbia* around, nothing happened. Again he worked the controls. Again *Columbia* did not respond. Many people would have panicked, but Collins remained calm and kept pushing the knob until at last the computer understood his instructions. He then skillfully piloted *Columbia* to face *Eagle* and locked them together, nose-to-nose. Finally, the used-up third-stage engine fell off. *Columbia* and *Eagle* were ready for their three-day voyage to the moon.

Inside the spacecraft, the men helped one another out of their uncomfortable space suits. The heavy suits cost almost one million dollars each and were scientifically designed to protect the astronauts and maintain their body temperatures. They were made of the strongest fabric known, since the slightest little tear at the wrong time would have meant death for the wearer.

Ten hours after the launch, the astronauts did a TV broadcast back to Earth. They showed everyone at home what it was like inside *Columbia* and even pointed the camera at the Earth to show people what their planet looked like from space!

The whole world was watching in amazement. But no one could know how it really felt to be so far away from the planet that held every single thing the three men knew and loved. To the astronauts, the entire Earth looked like no more than a fragile painted ornament hanging in a dark, vast universe. But on that living, spinning ball were their families, their friends, and all the people they had never met all over the world. How different it must have been to see the Earth without all the man-made lines that divide nations on our maps and globes.

The astronauts helped one another out of their heavy space suits.

For the next three days, the astronauts watched the Earth slowly shrink as they raced farther and farther away from it. First it filled the entire window of the spaceship. Then one of them might look again out the window—after charging batteries, dumping waste water, or changing fuel cells—and see that the Earth was only half the size it had been before. He would sleep and wake up, and it would look smaller still. Eventually, he could blot it out entirely by holding up his thumb.

By the third day of the mission, the moon's gravity pulled the craft with more force than the Earth's gravity. The moon was looming outside the windows. Michael Collins said, "It was a totally different moon than I had ever seen before. The moon that I knew from old was a yellow, flat disk, and this was a huge three-dimensional sphere, almost a ghostly blue-tinged sort of pale white. It didn't seem like a very friendly or welcoming place. It made one wonder whether we should be invading its domain or not."

By the third day of the mission, the moon's gravity pulled the spacecraft with more force than the Earth's gravity.

Neil Armstrong and Buzz Aldrin boarded *Eagle* and made last-minute checks.

On the fourth day, the moon completely filled the spacecraft window. Part of the moon was lit brightly by Earthshine—sunshine reflected off the Earth onto the moon's surface. Neil Armstrong said that the Earthshine coming through his window was bright enough to read a book by.

The astronauts prepared for the dangerous task of locking the ship into the moon's gravity. For *Apollo 11* to orbit the moon properly, they had to fire *Columbia*'s rocket engine at just the right speed. If the engine did not fire, *Apollo 11* would loop around the moon and zoom back toward Earth.

If it fired too powerfully, they would lose control and crash onto the moon's surface.

The rocket fired perfectly! *Apollo 11* orbited the moon thirteen times while the astronauts prepared for *Eagle*'s solo flight. After getting some sleep, Armstrong and Aldrin climbed into their space suits and crawled through the small tunnel that led to *Eagle*'s hatch. They strapped themselves into *Eagle* and performed the last-minute checks. All three men held their breath as Collins pushed the button that would release *Eagle* from *Columbia*.

Slowly, tiny *Eagle* floated away from the larger craft and began drifting gently toward the moon's surface. Collins checked *Eagle* for problems through the window of *Columbia*. Then, seeing that everything looked good, he left *Eagle* and continued guiding *Columbia* on its orbit around the moon. Armstrong radioed to the people on Earth, "The *Eagle* has wings."

Eagle was to land in an area on the moon called the Sea of Tranquility. The spot was chosen because it was flat and open and offered the best surface for a safe landing. If *Eagle* landed on a hill, or if one of its legs landed on a boulder and it toppled over, it would not be able to take off. There would be no way for Collins to rescue the other astronauts if that happened.

Were Neil Armstrong and Buzz Aldrin afraid as they floated down toward the moon? Even if *Eagle* landed in a flat area, there was the possibility for disaster. Some scientists believed that the layer of dust on the moon's surface was dangerously deep. They worried that the whole *Eagle* would just sink under the surface and never be seen again, or that the men would fall into the deep dust and be buried alive.

Eagle broke away from *Columbia* and headed for the moon.

The two astronauts inside *Eagle* had been preparing for the historic moment just ahead of them their whole lives. Buzz Aldrin had always loved anything to do with flying. His dad had been an expert pilot and a friend of Orville Wright and Charles Lindbergh, two of the most famous pilots in history. And his mom's maiden name was Marian Moon!

Neil Armstrong had also loved flight as a boy. He had built an elaborate wind tunnel in his family's basement so he could test his model airplanes. He had been so anxious to start flying that he earned his pilot's license before he was old enough even to get a driver's license!

As *Eagle* continued its course, Michael Collins was alone in *Columbia* for the first time. What was he thinking about as he circled the moon without his two friends? Any slight equipment failure could mean tragedy for *Eagle*. Collins would have to leave and head back to Earth all alone. The moon's back side was completely dark. The only way Collins could tell where the surface began was to see where the stars stopped. He knew that *Columbia* was orbiting the moon sixty miles above its surface, and he trusted that he wouldn't hit anything. Still, the scary thought occurred to him that he was blindly skimming along just barely above an alien land.

Michael Collins was alone for the first time, circling the moon in *Columbia*.

Meanwhile, *Eagle* moved closer and closer to the moon. But as Armstrong looked out the window, he froze. The computer was taking *Eagle* to the chosen landing site, but Armstrong could now see that the spot was covered with boulders the size of cars! There was no way *Eagle* could land safely there. Quickly he grabbed the rocket control handle to stop the computer and began operating the landing system on his own. He searched the area for a smooth place to set down. *Eagle* was only one hundred feet above the surface, and the landing engine was almost out of fuel.

With just moments to spare, Neil Armstrong landed *Eagle* safely on the moon's surface.

Back on Earth, the mission controllers did not know about the boulders. "Sixty seconds!" they radioed. That meant that *Eagle* had only one minute to land before it ran out of fuel. With no time to spare, Armstrong located an area several hundred yards to the right that looked like a good landing surface. He skillfully piloted *Eagle* to the spot. Dust shot up around the lunar module, making it hard for the astronauts to see. Had they touched down? Armstrong and Aldrin looked at each other in the now perfectly still *Eagle*. The cloud of dust moved away. The two men smiled. "Tranquility base here," Armstrong said into the radio. "The *Eagle* has landed."

An eerie landscape filled the window. Armstrong and Aldrin were scheduled to rest for four hours, but they were much too excited to wait another moment. They ate a quick meal and started getting ready for their moon walk. Temperatures on the moon range from -247 to 212 degrees Fahrenheit. That's cold enough to instantly freeze a human's blood and hot enough to boil it. There is no oxygen to breathe on the moon. The men's lives depended completely upon their space suits.

Armstrong snapped shut the final seal of his helmet and slowly backed out of *Eagle*'s hatch. A camera on the base of *Eagle* allowed millions of people on Earth to watch on their televisions as he carefully stepped down the nine rungs of the ladder. Armstrong could see that *Eagle*'s footpads had sunk only a few inches into the dust. The surface of the moon seemed to be safe.

Then Neil Armstrong took the most famous step in history—and made the first-ever footprint in the moon's soil. He said into the radio in his helmet, "That's one small step for man, one giant leap for mankind." He had planned to say, "That's one small step for a man," but he was so excited and nervous, he left out the word "a."

Neil Armstrong took the most famous step in history when he made the first-ever footprint in the moon's soil.

All over the world, people watched and cheered as Armstrong bounded lightly from one foot to the other across the landing area. The moon's low gravity made his walk seem more like a joyful skip as he collected moon rocks that had rested undisturbed since before the time of the dinosaurs. It was so silent inside his space suit, he could hear his own heart beating. "It has a stark beauty all its own," he said. "It's different, but it's very pretty out here."

Soon Buzz Aldrin joined him on the surface, and the two men practiced different ways of moving about. They showed the TV viewers on Earth a plaque they would leave on the moon. It said, "Here Men from the planet Earth first set foot upon the Moon, July 1969 AD. We came in peace for all mankind." The plaque was signed by each of the crew members and by the President of the United States, Richard Nixon.

Buzz Aldrin joined Neil Armstrong, and they practiced different ways of walking on the moon.

The astronauts planted an American flag on the moon and received a phone call from President Nixon back on Earth. "For one priceless moment, in the whole history of man," said the President, "all the people of Earth are truly one. One in their pride in what you have done. And one in our prayers that you will return safely to Earth. As you talk to us from the Sea of Tranquility, it requires us to redouble our efforts to bring peace and tranquility to Earth."

Armstrong and Aldrin conducted scientific experiments and collected rock samples from the moon. Then, less than three hours after first stepping on the lunar surface, the two men reluctantly climbed back into *Eagle* and closed the hatch. They slept restlessly for a few hours and then fired the ascent engine that launched *Eagle* away from the moon to meet up with the waiting *Columbia*.

After three hours, the astronauts got back into *Eagle* and blasted off.

Eagle joined with *Columbia*. The three astronauts were going home.

Collins was very happy to be reunited with his friends. Since there was no TV on *Columbia*, he was one of the few people who did not get to see the activity on the moon. As *Columbia's* engine was fired once more, Neil Armstrong, Buzz Aldrin, and Michael Collins watched the beautiful, welcoming Earth rise up over the lunar horizon. They were going home.